LIFE-CHANGING
COMPOUND BUTTERS
IN 3 MINUTES FLAT

TABLE OF CONTENTS

Compound Butter

What's compound butter? I thought you'd never ask! It's merely plain butter mixed with other ingredients, often in some very interesting combinations, for use as a topping, spread, or just to let melt over a protein or vegetable. That's it, but oh what melting mounds of deliciousness they are. What could be better than butter, rich and silky, packed with the flavors of spices, aromatics, cheeses, nuts, fruits, sugars, and specialty condiments? They're simply irresistible, and once made can yield up to eight portions.

Compound butters can enhance meats, poultry, fish, and even brunch items in the same way that sauces, spreads, or toppings would. In this book, recipes for all three of these ideas will be implemented. From classic to exotic, you can make absolutely all of your meals more interesting. Even home-delivery meal programs will benefit from a mound of this lip-smacking goodness. The main thing to remember is that the quality of your finished product will depend completely upon the quality of your ingredients. Don't skimp on quality.

Enhance many plates at once, or use your compound butter over many meals. Even the most fragile ones will keep for a week in the fridge, and much longer in the freezer. So what have you got to lose? Dig in and find a flavor combination that makes *your* mouth water, then let it bring your dishes to life.

~Grace Légere

An Organized Pantry Equals Fast Compounds

Items to have on hand

A small glass or metal bowl approximately 6" to 8" in diameter, a fork, a spoon, a rubber spatula, a set of measuring spoons, a measuring cup, a cutting board, a cook's rasp for proper zesting of fresh citrus skin, and some plastic wrap. *(Prior ingredient preparation may require a chef's knife, a zester, cheese grater, measuring cup, colander, and paper towels depending on the fresh ingredients used.)*

The standard measurement

These recipes call for one stick of butter [½ c. or ¼ lb.] to make one roll of compound butter yielding eight portions. If you want less simply half it, or for more simply double it.

Salted or unsalted butter?

Each recipe will specify which to use so be sure to look for it. Compound butters with salty ingredients going in will not need any help in the way of butter that is already salted. Unsalted "sweet" butter will be specified when required.

Prepare all ingredients before you begin

First, make sure your butter is softened but not melted. Dried herbs (generally not recommended unless noted) can be used "as is" of course, but fresh herbs must be de-stemmed and chopped. *(Thyme, oregano, and rosemary will release their leaves from the stem more readily if you pull them backwards with two fingers.)* Fresh fruits are called for in several of my recipes. They must be finely chopped and separated from their watery juice by draining in a colander and then squeezing in a strong paper towel. Not only will this prevent a compound butter that won't hold together, it will also concentrate the flavor of the fruit in your finished product. Whenever jam or preserves can be used instead, do it. Your finished product will be better blended because of it. When ground nuts are called for, a food processor will make quick work of it. Stop pulsing when the nuts are mealy or you can end up with a gooey "nut butter" instead.

Ingredients that are already washed, chopped, and drained, means your preparation time of the actual compound butter will be super fast.

Wrapping & Shaping

The best technique for shaping your compound butter into a log shape (for slicing later) is to place the entire blended bowlful onto a 12″ sheet of plastic wrap. Then, as you roll, cover it completely with the wrap while using pressure with your hands in order to urge the butter into a longer log. Twisting the wrap at both ends will insure it is sealed and ready for chilling.

For chilled storage

All of these compound butters can be kept chilled in a refrigerator for a week or so. When ready to eat, bring to room temperature for five minutes and then slice into round discs by cutting with a sharp knife run under hot water. Then simply place the discs onto the proteins or vegetables that you wish to enhance.

Note: Chilled, log-shaped compounds serve two purposes: for the convenience of making it ahead and storing it, or to slow the "melt time" thereby improving the presentation of a plated dish. If you are pressed for time, skip the plastic wrap and rolling technique altogether and simply place your bowl of blended compound butter into the refrigerator to set up for a five to ten minutes. Just before serving, scoop by spoonfuls right onto the waiting food.

Freeze for prolonged storage

Compound Butters keep well in the freezer up to two months...simply cover the plastic-wrapped logs in foil before freezing.

To use, thaw in the refrigerator overnight and then let it come slightly to room temperature for five minutes before slicing or scooping into individual ramekins. *(See chapter on Brunch Butters for butter spreads.)*

Special decorative molds

To elevate the look of your finished compound butter, decorative molds are available for purchase online. They assure a very professional look but aren't necessary for a successful compound butter.

How to make homemade butter

Pour chilled, heavy cream into a clean mixing bowl and beat past the point of whipping cream… the next stage will be silky, rich, unsalted butter. Simply drain the excess water that has accumulated and enjoy. *Many a chef has made butter by accident when whipping heavy cream.*

Know my cooking abbreviations

t.   means *teaspoon*
T.   means *tablespoon*
c.   means *cup*
oz.   means *fluid ounces*
lbs.   means *pounds*

French Butters

The French have always appreciated fine food, especially when it's highlighted with authentic European ingredients. Here are several compound butters that will bring France to your table.

- **The simple instructions:**
In a small bowl, blend all ingredients together with a fork. Once well combined, allow to set up in the refrigerator for a few minutes until ready to plate. Eight servings.

For future use, place the entire bowl of compound butter onto a sheet of plastic wrap for forming. Once it's completely covered in the wrap, roll the mound of compound butter into a log shape for chilling and slicing later with a hot knife.

Morel, Garlic, & Tarragon Butter
Re-hydrated Morel mushrooms pack a punch of earthy flavor

1 stick salted butter, slightly softened
1 t. chopped fresh tarragon
1 to 2 cloves of fresh garlic, finely minced, to taste
2 T. finely chopped, re-hydrated dried mushrooms (Morel preferred)
> *Dried mushrooms are more intense in flavor and can be easily re-hydrated in a bowl of warm water for 15 minutes, then drained, patted dry, and finely chopped*

Port Wine & Chèvre Butter
Heady with the strong flavor of wine and goat cheese, pair this one with red meat

1 stick salted butter, slightly softened
3 T. softened goat cheese, with or without an herb coating
2 T. port wine
Pinch of freshly ground pepper, to taste

Sage & Kumquat Butter
Pork tenderloin medallions yearn for this earthy and citrusy combination

1 stick salted butter, slightly softened
1 T. finely chopped fresh sage leaves
3 fresh kumquats with skin, *finely chopped and drained of excess moisture on a paper towel*

Dark Cherry & Port Wine Butter
The French have used cherries in their cuisine for centuries –
try this one on any poultry

1 stick salted butter, slightly softened
2 T. cherry preserves
> *You may also use fresh, pitted dark cherries, very finely chopped and squeezed free of excess moisture in a paper towel, or frozen cherries which have been properly thawed*
1½ T. port wine

Rosemary, Garlic, Parsley & Mint Butter
Simply superb on lamb chops

1 stick salted butter, slightly softened
1 T. finely chopped fresh parsley
1 T. finely chopped fresh mint leaves
2 t. minced fresh rosemary leaves – *remove leaves from stem by pulling backwards*
1 or 2 cloves fresh garlic, finely minced, to taste

Sage & Apple Calvados Butter
Cooking roast pork? Splurge on some French apple brandy for a delicious topping

1 stick salted butter, slightly softened
1 t. finely chopped fresh sage leaves
1 t. finely chopped parsley
1 t. apple-butter condiment
1 T. Calvados brandy

Shallot & Dijon Butter
These strong flavorings will stand up to any red meat

1 stick salted butter, slightly softened
1 t. finely chopped fresh shallot
1 T. grainy Dijon mustard

Honey & Dijon Mustard Butter
Lip-smacking goodness on any chicken

1 stick salted butter, slightly softened
1½ T. honey
1 T. Dijon mustard

Lemon, Parsley, & Marjoram Butter
Clean and tart, try this one on seafood

1 stick salted butter, slightly softened
1 T. finely chopped fresh marjoram
2 T. chopped fresh parsley
1 T. grated fresh lemon zest

Italian Butters

Italy's cuisine has contributed much to the world of food, and that nation's distinct flavors lend the perfect touch to compound butters.

- **The simple instructions:**

In a small bowl, blend all ingredients together with a fork. Once well combined, allow to set up in the refrigerator for a few minutes until ready to plate. Eight servings.

For future use, place the entire bowl of compound butter onto a sheet of plastic wrap for forming. Once it's completely covered in the wrap, roll the mound of compound butter into a log shape for chilling and slicing later with a hot knife.

Basil, Sundried Tomato, & Black Pepper Butter
This one will bring Italian flavors to any dish

1 stick salted butter, slightly softened
2 T. chopped fresh basil
Good pinch of freshly ground black pepper
2 T. finely chopped, re-hydrated sundried tomatoes

> *Sundried tomatoes are intense in flavor and can be easily re-hydrated in a bowl of warm water for 15 minutes, then drained, patted dry, and finely chopped – if you have the ones packed in oil, drain well on a paper towel after chopping. (A food processor makes quick work of sundried tomatoes which can be difficult to cut)*

Green Olive & Roasted Red Pepper Butter
These hearty Italian flavors can top anything... try this on freshly baked bread

1 stick unsalted butter, slightly softened
2 t. green olives finely chopped *and patted dry of excess moisture*
2 t. roasted red peppers finely chopped *and patted dry of its brine*

Oregano, Garlic, & Hot Pepper Flakes Butter
The spicy flavors of the Abruzzo region perk up both meat and fish

1 stick salted butter, slightly softened
1 T. finely chopped fresh oregano, or 2 t. dried oregano
2 cloves fresh garlic, finely minced
¼ t. dried hot red pepper flakes, or less if you prefer it milder

Orange, Raisin, and Roasted Red Peppers Butter
Sicilian grandmas know the amazing flavor this combo brings to both poultry and fish

1 stick salted butter, slightly softened
1 T. finely chopped raisins, *softened in warm water then drained and patted dry before chopping*
2 T. finely chopped roasted red peppers, *drained well of their packing oil or brine on a paper towel*
2 t. grated fresh orange zest

Truffle Butter
Truffles are very expensive but many people feel they are worth every penny

1 stick salted butter, slightly softened
1 t. finely chopped fresh truffles (or jar/prepared)
   If they're out of season, you can use ½ t. truffle oil, to taste (This oil is strong so go easy on it!)

Romano, Garlic, & Lemon Butter
Robust sheep's milk cheese and citrus blend beautifully with garlic for a Roman treat

1 stick unsalted butter, slightly softened
1 or 2 cloves fresh garlic, finely minced, to taste
1 t. grated fresh lemon zest
¼ c. finely grated Pecorino Romano cheese
Pinch of salt, if desired

Morel, Garlic, & Sundried Tomato Butter
Dried mushrooms & tomatoes are a heavenly match

1 stick salted butter, slightly softened
1 or 2 cloves fresh garlic, finely minced, to taste
2 T. finely chopped, re-hydrated sundried tomatoes
> *Sundried tomatoes are intense in flavor and can be easily re-hydrated in a bowl of warm water for 15 minutes, then drained, patted dry, and finely chopped – if you have the ones packed in oil, drain well on a paper towel after chopping. (A food processor makes quick work of sundried tomatoes which can be difficult to cut)*

2 T. finely chopped, re-hydrated dried mushrooms (Morel preferred)
> *Dried mushrooms are more intense in flavor and can be easily re-hydrated in a bowl of warm water for 10 minutes, then drained, patted dry and chopped*

Lemon, Oregano, Capers, & Parmesan Butter
The distinctive taste of aged Italian cheese and citrus pairs well with poultry

1 stick unsalted butter, slightly softened
2 t. finely chopped fresh oregano, or 1 t. dried oregano
1 t. finely chopped capers patted dry of their brine
1 t. grated fresh lemon zest
2 T. finely grated Parmesan cheese

Pine nut, Parmesan, Garlic, & Basil Butter
Bring the flavor of classic pesto to your favorite protein or vegetable

1 stick unsalted butter, slightly softened
1 T. toasted, chopped pine nuts
2 T. finely chopped fresh basil leaves – *a thin chiffonade cut of this herb will work fine*
1 to 2 cloves fresh garlic, finely minced, to taste
¼ c. finely grated Parmesan cheese

Cacio e Pepe Butter
The flavors of this famous Roman pasta dish make a memorable compound butter

1 stick unsalted butter, slightly softened
1 or 2 cloves fresh garlic, finely minced, to taste
2 T. finely grated Romano cheese
½ t. freshly ground black pepper
Pinch of salt if desired – Romano cheese can be very salty

Balsamic & Roasted Garlic Butter
The natural sweetness in roasted garlic compliments the mild taste of real Balsamic

1 stick salted butter, slightly softened
2 t. aged Balsamic vinegar
3 to 4 cloves of roasted garlic (1 T. of garlic total)
> *Roasting a whole head of garlic is easy. Simply slice ½ inch off the entire top with a serrated knife and then wrap it tightly in foil. Bake in a preheated 400°F (205°C) oven for 35 minutes. Cool completely before unwrapping it. The soft, oozy garlic can be squeezed right out into a measuring spoon.*

Sundried Tomato & Romano Cheese Butter
Earthy and rich, this is a flavor pairing made in heaven

1 stick salted butter, slightly softened
¼ c. finely grated Romano cheese
2 T. finely chopped, re-hydrated sundried tomatoes
> *Sundried tomatoes are intense in flavor and can be easily re-hydrated in a bowl of warm water for 15 minutes, then drained, patted dry, and finely chopped — if you have the ones packed in oil, drain well on a paper towel after chopping. (A food processor makes quick work of sundried tomatoes which can be difficult to cut.)*

Asian Inspired Butters

Exotic Asian-inspired combinations add an exquisite taste to your dishes. Try these on your favorite protein or vegetable for an unexpected flavor profile.

- **The simple instructions:**

In a small bowl, blend all ingredients together with a fork. Once well combined, allow to set up in the refrigerator for a few minutes until ready to plate. Eight servings.

For future use, place the entire bowl of compound butter onto a sheet of plastic wrap for forming. Once it's completely covered in the wrap, roll the mound of compound butter into a log shape for chilling and slicing later with a hot knife.

Sesame, Ginger, & Garlic Butter
Classic Chinese flavors pack a punch of deliciousness on any protein

1 stick salted butter, slightly softened
1 T. sesame oil
1 t. fresh ginger flesh, grated or finely minced – *its outer skin can be easily scraped off with a spoon*
1 clove fresh garlic, finely minced
1 t. toasted sesame seeds
Pinch of salt, to taste

Chinese Five Spice & Garlic Butter
This exotic combo will dress up even the simplest chicken or pork

1 stick unsalted butter, slightly softened
1 to 2 t. Chinese Five-Spice powder, to taste
1 or 2 cloves fresh garlic, finely minced, to taste
1 T. chopped fresh chives

Lemon, Mint, Garlic, & Cilantro Butter
Bring these famous Vietnamese flavors to your chicken, fish, or lamb

1 stick salted butter, slightly softened
1 T. finely chopped fresh mint leaves
1 T. finely chopped fresh cilantro
1 T. grated fresh lemon zest
1 to 2 cloves fresh garlic, finely minced, to taste

Mango, Cilantro, & Hot Pepper Flakes Butter
Spicy & sweet, you'll love this exotic Southeast Asian-flavored butter

1 stick salted butter, slightly softened
1 T. finely chopped fresh cilantro
¼ t. dried hot red pepper flakes, less if you prefer a milder compound
2 T. fresh mango flesh, finely chopped *and squeezed of excess moisture in a paper towel*

Molasses, Ginger, & Soy Butter
The rich flavors of this combo will have your guests begging for seconds

1 stick unsalted butter, slightly softened
1 T. soy sauce
2 t. molasses syrup
1 t. fresh ginger flesh, grated or finely minced – *its outer skin can be easily scraped off with a spoon*

Ginger, Scallion, & Sesame Butter
The nutty flavor of sesame pairs beautifully with fresh ginger

1 stick salted butter, slightly softened
1 T. sesame oil
1 t. fresh ginger flesh, grated or finely minced – *its outer skin can be easily scraped off with a spoon*
½ fresh scallion, finely chopped
1 T. honey
1 t. toasted sesame seeds

Cashew, Honey, & Lime Butter

Bring the taste of the Philippines home with these exotic flavors

1 stick salted butter, slightly softened
2 T. ground, roasted cashews
1 T. honey
1½ t. good quality fish sauce
2 t. grated fresh lime zest

Mint, Lemon, & Honey Butter

Think these flavor profiles won't compliment each other? Think again!

1 stick salted butter, slightly softened
1 T. fresh chopped fresh mint leaves
1 T. honey
1 T. grated fresh lemon zest

Brunch Butters

Brunch butters are better when whipped with beaters, but it's not required…. just makes for a lighter consistency and spreadability.

- **The *special* instructions for these are simple:**

In a mixing bowl, beat softened butter for approximately two minutes on a medium-high speed until light and fluffy. Add all other ingredients one at a time until blended. *If you intend to use any of these as a spread for muffins, biscuits, or other baked goods, simply offer it up in individual ramekins.*

Six servings.

- When making fruit-filled compound butters, jams and preserves incorporate much easier than chopped fruit! You can use either homemade jam or a good quality one from the store. If you decide to chance it and use chopped fresh fruit, remember that it must be drained of all juices in a colander or squeezed in strong paper towels before incorporating into the butter.

- If an electric mixer is not available, blend all ingredients together in a small bowl with a fork, adding them in the order given.

- Once well combined, use immediately by 1 tablespoon scoops into the ramekins or directly onto food, or store in the refrigerator for a few minutes until ready to plate.

Note: For future use, place your brunch butter in a plastic container with a lid and refrigerate. When ready to use, let come to room temperature for at least ten minutes for easier scooping.

Classic Strawberry Butter
The quintessential spread for biscuits, muffins, and waffles

1 stick salted butter, slightly softened and beaten in a mixer with the other ingredient
2 T. good quality strawberry jam

Pecan, Brown Sugar, & Cinnamon Butter
Southern hospitality never tasted so good

1 stick salted butter, slightly softened and beaten in a mixer with the other ingredients
2 T. ground, roasted pecans
1 T. brown sugar
¼ t. ground cinnamon

Cinnamon & Sugar Butter
The flavors of childhood combine to make a luscious spread or compound "melt"

1 stick salted butter, slightly softened and beaten in a mixer with the other ingredients
½ t. ground cinnamon
½ t. granulated white sugar

Maple & Cashew Butter
An elegant breakfast combo

1 stick salted butter, slightly softened and beaten in a mixer with the other ingredients
2 T. ground roasted cashews
1 T. pure maple syrup *–the "maple flavored" stuff does not have enough intensity for this compound*

Raspberry Butter
Sweet and sour deliciousness

1 stick unsalted butter, slightly softened and beaten in a mixer with the other ingredient
2 T. good quality raspberry jam, with or without seeds

Cashew Compound Butter
Ground cashews make butter even more buttery!

1 stick salted butter, slightly softened and beaten in a mixer with the other ingredient
3 T. finely chopped or ground roasted cashews

Maple & Chocolate Chip Butter
Chopped dark chocolate and real maple syrup will transform your pancakes

1 stick salted butter, slightly softened and beaten in a mixer with the other ingredients
2-3 T. finely chopped chocolate or mini chips
1 t. brown sugar
1 T. pure maple syrup *–the "maple flavored" stuff does not have enough intensity for this compound*

Fig, Pecan, & Brown Sugar Butter
Introduce fresh figs and nuts to your favorite brunch breads

1 stick salted butter, slightly softened and beaten in a mixer with the other ingredients
1½ T. ground roasted pecans
1 T. brown sugar
2 T. finely chopped fresh fig flesh– *its outer skin can be used only if it's the thin skin variety*

Sweet Gorgonzola & Honey Butter
This famous Italian combo will elevate any brunch item

1 stick unsalted butter, slightly softened and beaten in a mixer with the other ingredients
2 T. sweet gorgonzola cheese
2 T. honey

Bacon & Brown Sugar Butter
Spread some sweet and salty harmony on your freshly baked breakfast breads

1 stick unsalted butter, slightly softened and beaten in a mixer with the other ingredients
1 T. brown sugar
1 ½ T. finely chopped cooked bacon

Bloody Mary Butter
This unique spread will be the star of your brunch party

1 stick salted butter, slightly softened and beaten in a mixer with the other ingredients
1-2 T. spicy tomato juice (or Bloody Mary mix) *Add slowly while mixing!*
¼ t. celery seeds
1 t. grated fresh lemon zest
¼ t. hot pepper sauce, to taste
Pinch of freshly ground black pepper, to taste

Honey & Almond Apricot Butter
The sweetness of honey blends with juicy apricots for a tasty spread

1 stick unsalted butter, slightly softened and beaten in a mixer with the other ingredients
2 T. honey
2 T. good quality apricot jam
1 T. ground roasted almonds

Pumpkin Spice Butter
Just like grandma's homemade pumpkin pie, and perfect on pancakes

1 stick salted butter, slightly softened and beaten in a mixer with the other ingredients
1 T. brown sugar, beat into the butter
1 T. "Pumpkin Pie Spice" blend
1 T. canned pure packed pumpkin (optional)

Boysenberry Butter
What could be better than a tart, dark purple compound butter?

1 stick unsalted butter, slightly softened and beaten in a mixer with the other ingredients
2 T. good quality boysenberry jam
Pinch of salt if desired

Mango Butter
Quite simply the perfect tropical compound butter

1 stick unsalted butter, slightly softened and beaten in a mixer with the other ingredients
2 T. good quality mango preserves
Pinch of salt if desired

Key Lime Butter
The tropical tang of juicy Key limes will perk up your waffles

1 stick unsalted butter, slightly softened and beaten in a mixer with the other ingredients
2 T. cream cheese
2 T. powdered confectioner's sugar
1 T. freshly grated key lime zest – *Key limes are juicy but small, so get enough to yield zest!*

Kiwi Butter
Tangy and juicy, try this one melting over French toast.

1 stick unsalted butter, slightly softened and beaten in a mixer with the other ingredients
2 T. powdered confectioner's sugar *–beat into the butter before adding the fruit*
½ c. fresh kiwi flesh, *finely chopped and squeezed of excess moisture in a paper towel*

Raspberry Cheesecake Butter
Cream cheese adds a rich, dessert quality to this wonderful compound

1 stick unsalted butter, slightly softened and beaten in a mixer with the other ingredients
3 T. cream cheese
2 T. good quality raspberry jam

Honey Butter

The quintessential sweet butter spread for any baked good

1 stick salted butter, slightly softened and beaten in a mixer
2 T. honey drizzled into the butter while mixing

Specialty Butters

Your tastebuds will sing when they get ahold of any of these amazing flavor combinations. Use your imagination to pair them with a worthy protein, or even a favorite bakery item.

- **The simple instructions:**

In a small bowl, blend all ingredients together with a fork. Once well combined, allow to set up in the refrigerator for a few minutes just until ready to plate. Eight servings.

For future use, place the entire bowl of compound butter onto a sheet of plastic wrap for forming. Once it's completely covered in the wrap, roll the mound of compound butter into a log shape for chilling and slicing later with a hot knife.

- If you want to use these as a spread for muffins, biscuits, or other baked goods, simply offer it up in small, individual ramekins.

Honey, Mustard, Scallion, & Parsley Butter
My family loves this one on poultry or fish

1 stick salted butter, slightly softened
1 T. honey
1 T. prepared mustard
2 T. finely chopped parsley
1 fresh scallion, chopped

Peppadew Peppers & Parsley Butter
The mildly hot, piquant flavor will wake up any protein

1 stick salted butter, slightly softened
2 T. finely chopped mild Peppadew peppers, drained and patted dry of their excess brine
1 T. finely chopped fresh parsley

Smoky Almonds, Blue Cheese, & Chive Butter
This combo will provide a memorable punch to your palate – try it on grilled steak

1 stick unsalted butter, slightly softened
1½ T. finely chopped or crushed smoked almonds
2 t. finely chopped fresh chives
2 T. good quality blue cheese – *Roquefort preferred*

Pepper Jelly & Cream Cheese Butter
Tangy creaminess and mild heat create the perfect biscuit topper

1 stick salted butter, slightly softened
2 T. green or red pepper jelly – *Can be found in specialty stores*
2 T. cream cheese

Spicy Jerk & Mango Butter
Sweet, spicy and very addictive on grilled chicken breast

1 stick unsalted butter, slightly softened
2 T. good quality mango preserves
1-2 t. Jerk seasoning, to taste

Mint, Cumin & Lemon Butter
Unusual to be sure, this one brings an exotic South American flavor to any dish

1 stick salted butter, slightly softened
1 T. finely chopped fresh mint leaves
½ t. ground cumin
1 T. grated fresh lemon zest

Chili Powder & Sundried Tomato Butter
Hearty Southwest flavors raise your compound butter to the next level

1 stick salted butter, slightly softened
2 T. finely chopped, re-hydrated sundried tomatoes
> *Sundried tomatoes are intense in flavor and can be easily re-hydrated in a bowl of warm water for 15 minutes, then drained, patted dry, and finely chopped – if you have the ones packed in oil, drain well on a paper towel after chopping. (A food processor makes quick work of sundried tomatoes which can be difficult to cut.)*

½ t. ground cumin
¼ t. chili powder

The Magic of Peru Butter
Mimic the taste of the Peruvian herb "Huacatay" with this special blend

1 stick salted butter, slightly softened
1 T. finely chopped fresh basil
2 t. chopped fresh tarragon
2 t. chopped fresh mint leaves
1 T. grated fresh lime zest
½ t. ground coriander

Creamy Chive & Bacon Butter
The smoky saltiness goes great on beef, poultry, or homemade biscuits

1 stick unsalted butter, slightly softened
2 T. cream cheese
2 T. finely chopped cooked bacon
1 T. finely chopped fresh chives

Fresh Jalapeño & Bacon Butter
Spicy and meaty, this butter can be enjoyed on just about anything

1 stick unsalted butter, slightly softened
2 T. finely chopped cooked bacon
1 T. finely chopped fresh jalapeño peppers
> *Remove all seeds and white pith from the peppers, then drain off any excess moisture on a paper towel. Be sure to wash your hands well with soap afterwards, and be careful not to touch your eyes while working with the hot peppers!*

Lox, Dill & Capers Butter
Kind of Russian, kind of Jewish... try this blend as a spread on freshly baked bread

1 stick salted butter, slightly softened
2 T. cream cheese
1 t. finely chopped fresh dill
1 t. chopped capers, drained of their brine
1½ T. finely chopped lox (brine-cured salmon)
  Smoked salmon may be used in place of the brine-cured variety

Classic Compound Butters

Easy-to-find ingredients blended together in familiar combinations are sure to please even the fussiest palates.

- **The simple instructions:**
In a small bowl, blend all ingredients together with a fork. Once well combined, allow to set up in the refrigerator for a few minutes until ready to plate. Eight servings.

For future use, place the entire bowl of compound butter onto a sheet of plastic wrap for forming. Once it's completely covered in the wrap, roll the mound of compound butter into a log shape for chilling and slicing later with a hot knife.

Lemon & Chive Butter
The classic combo for enhancing any fish or seafood

1 stick salted butter, slightly softened
1 T. finely chopped fresh chives
1 T. grated fresh lemon zest
Pinch of salt, to taste

Parsley, Sage, Rosemary, & Thyme Butter
This famous foursome is the perfect accent on roast pork

1 stick salted butter, slightly softened
1 T. finely chopped fresh parsley
½ t. finely chopped fresh rosemary – *remove leaves from stem by pulling backwards*
1 t. finely chopped fresh sage – *leaves only*
1 t. finely chopped fresh thyme – *remove leaves from stem by pulling backwards*

Lemon & Garlic Butter
The world's favorite compound butter for fish and seafood

1 stick salted butter, slightly softened
1 or 2 cloves fresh garlic, finely minced, to taste
1 T. grated fresh lemon zest
Pinch of salt, to taste
Pinch of ground pepper, to taste

Rosemary & Mint Butter
Slices of roast lamb only get better with this butter melting over it

1 stick salted butter, slightly softened
1 T. finely chopped rosemary – *remove leaves from stem by pulling backwards*
1 T. finely chopped fresh mint leaves

Lemon Thyme Butter
These two ingredients compliment each other perfectly

1 stick salted butter, slightly softened
1 t. finely chopped fresh thyme – *remove leaves from stem by pulling backwards*
1 T. grated fresh lemon zest

Curry & Parsley Butter
Fresh, with a hint of spice

1 stick salted butter, slightly softened
1 T. finely chopped fresh parsley
1 t. curry powder
Salt and pepper, to taste – *may not be necessary*

Easy "1 ingredient" Butters

By blending butter with even one ingredient, you can whip up a super-quick compound that boasts a clean, simple flavor profile.

- **The simple instructions:**
In a small bowl, blend all ingredients together with a fork. Once well combined, allow to set up in the refrigerator for a few minutes until ready to plate. Eight servings.

For future use, place the entire bowl of compound butter onto a sheet of plastic wrap for forming. Once it's completely covered in the wrap, roll the mound of compound butter into a log shape for chilling and slicing later with a hot knife.

Roasted Garlic Butter
Roasting the garlic first makes a huge difference in the taste

1 stick salted butter, slightly softened
3 to 4 cloves roasted garlic (1 T. of garlic total)
> *Roasting a whole head of garlic is easy. Simply slice ½ inch off the entire top with a serrated knife and then wrap it tightly in foil. Bake in a preheated 400°F (205°C) oven for 35 minutes. Cool completely before unwrapping it. The soft, oozy garlic can be squeezed right out into a measuring spoon.*

Fresh Garlic Butter
The classic! Use for making homemade garlic bread

1 stick salted butter, slightly softened
2 to 3 cloves fresh garlic, finely minced, to taste

Fresh Orange Butter
Try this surprising butter on warm tortillas

1 stick salted butter, slightly softened
1 T. grated fresh orange zest

Tarragon Butter
This delicious butter melted over peas is simply unforgettable

1 stick salted butter, slightly softened
1 T. chopped fresh tarragon
Pinch of ground pepper, to taste

Paprika Butter
The favorite spice of Hungarians adds smoky richness to silky butter

1 stick salted butter, slightly softened
1½ t. ground paprika

Shallot Butter
Finely minced shallot adds a garlicky-onion flavor to your favorite steak

1 stick salted butter, slightly softened
1 T. finely chopped fresh shallot
Pinch of ground pepper, to taste

Lemon Butter
Fish is always better with this classic topping

1 stick salted butter, slightly softened
1 T. grated fresh lemon zest

Grapefruit Butter
The dry tartness of grapefruit bursts with flavor in this compound butter

1 stick unsalted butter, slightly softened
1 T. grated fresh grapefruit zest

Bitter Orange Butter
Marmalade provides the perfect flavor in this easy compound

1 stick unsalted butter, slightly softened (and beaten in a mixer for fluffiness, if desired)
2 T. good quality orange marmalade

Dark Chocolate Chip Butter
A simple idea turns Pain Perdu into an elevated dessert

1 stick unsalted butter, slightly softened or beaten in a mixer until fluffy
1½ T. chopped dark chocolate or semi-sweet mini chips

Calling all cooks!

Thank you so much for your interest in my recipes. It was great fun bringing you these wonderful flavor combinations.

Please note that the star rating offered to you at the end of this book is for *metadata use only* and <u>does not affect this book's viewable online rating!</u> If you enjoyed *Life-Changing Compound Butters*, please take a moment to leave a short customer review on Amazon so that your rating will count for us. Even a few sentences would be helpful, and much appreciated.

~Grace

Books by Grace Légere

Life-Changing Salad Dressings In 3 Minutes Flat

Life-Changing Compound Butters In 3 Minutes Flat

Life-Changing Potato Salads In 30 Minutes Flat

Life-Changing Salsa Fresca In 30 Minutes Or Less

Made in the USA
San Bernardino, CA
17 February 2019